Who Needs Water?

Written by
Jill Atkins

All living things need water.

There is a lot of water on the planet.

Who can tell me where all the water we use comes from?

Water droplets rise from the sea and form clouds.

The wind makes the clouds drift onto the land.

Then the clouds drop the water on the land. That is rain.

The rain forms into streams and rivers. Some rivers go down to the sea.

And then it all starts again!

Some water goes into lakes.

This is a big lake where people have made a dam. The dam stops the water from running off and draining into the ground.

It keeps the water safe for people to use.

If we do not have much rain, the water level in the lake will go down.

Then we might not have much water.

Water from the lake travels in pipes into our homes.

We can drink fresh water that comes from the tap.

These children are having a bath.

We can wash the dishes in the sink or in the dishwasher. It is wise to slip on an apron to keep our outfit clean.

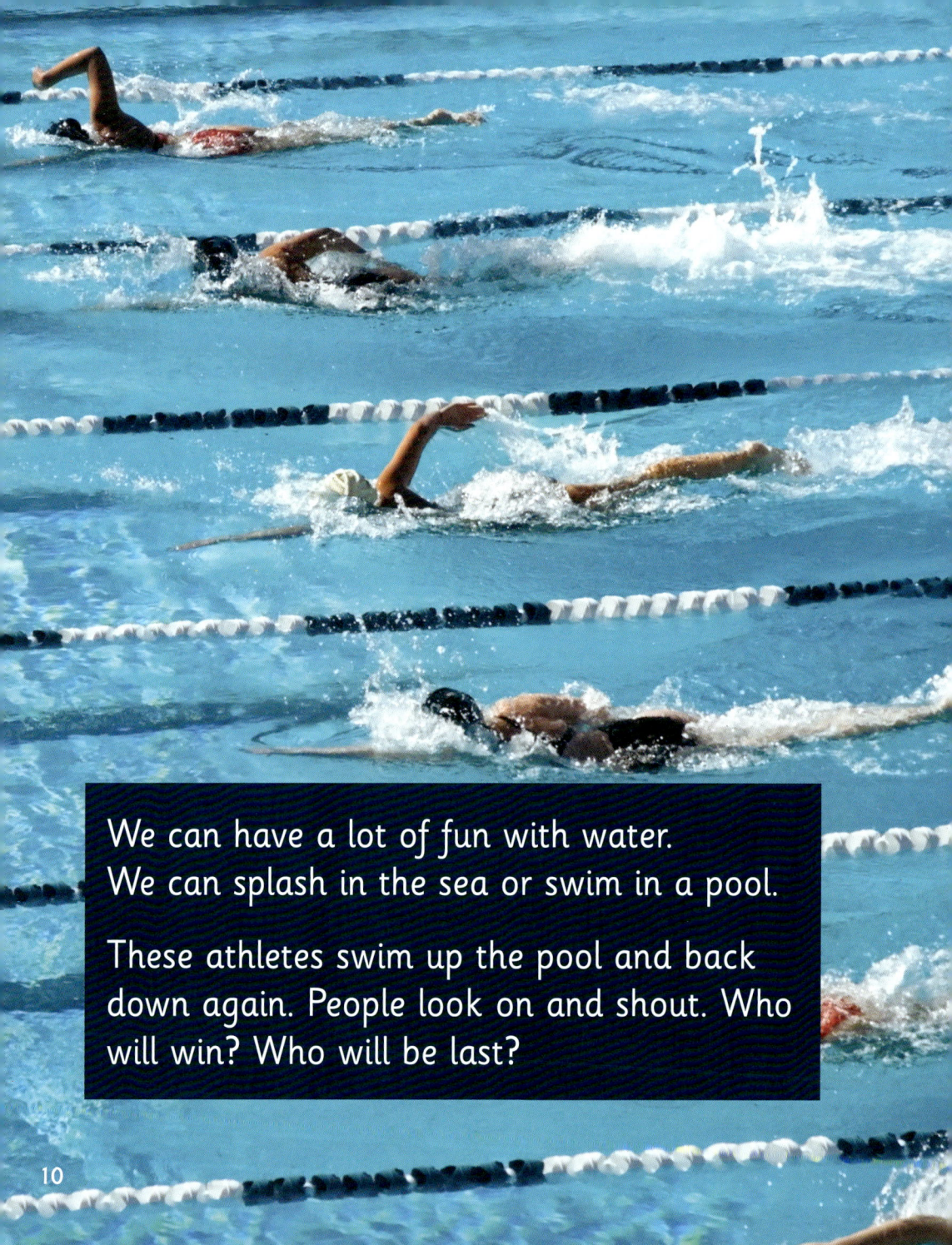

We can have a lot of fun with water.
We can splash in the sea or swim in a pool.

These athletes swim up the pool and back down again. People look on and shout. Who will win? Who will be last?

This speed boat is going fast too.

Where do you think these people are going?

Some parts of our planet are short of water.

There is not much rain and the hot sun dries the land so fast.

What will happen if this lake dries up?

Then the animals cannot wash or swim or drink. The grass and plants will die too, so the animals will have no water *and* no food.

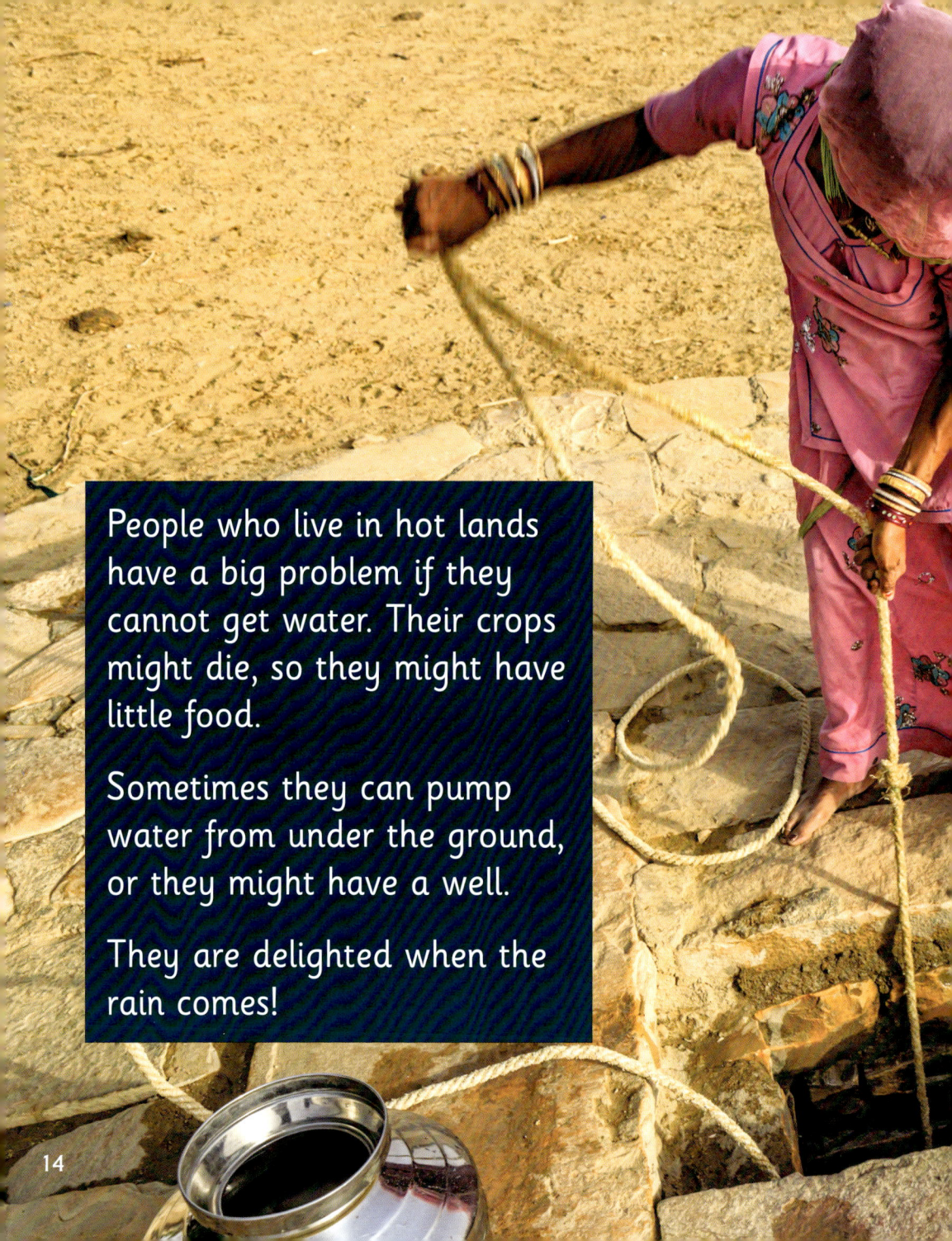

People who live in hot lands have a big problem if they cannot get water. Their crops might die, so they might have little food.

Sometimes they can pump water from under the ground, or they might have a well.

They are delighted when the rain comes!

Some people have no clean water.

Their water has lots of bugs in it. People might get sick if they drink this water.

Do you think clean water is the best thing on the planet?